WHINY BABY

THE HUGH MacLENNAN POETRY SERIES

Editors: Allan Hepburn and Carolyn Smart

Recent titles in the series

Whiny Baby

JULIE PAUL

McGill-Queen's University Press
Montreal & Kingston • London • Chicago

ISBN 978-0-2280-2074-5 (paper)
ISBN 978-0-2280-2075-2 (ePDF)
ISBN 978-0-2280-2076-9 (ePUB)

Legal deposit first quarter 2024
Bibliothèque nationale du Québec

Printed in Canada on acid-free paper that is 100% ancient forest free
(100% post-consumer recycled), processed chlorine free

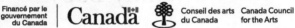

We acknowledge the support of the Canada Council for the Arts.

Nous remercions le Conseil des arts du Canada de son soutien.

McGill-Queen's University Press in Montreal is on land which long
served as a site of meeting and exchange amongst Indigenous Peoples,
including the Haudenosaunee and Anishinabeg nations. In Kingston
it is situated on the territory of the Haudenosaunee and Anishinaabek.
We acknowledge and thank the diverse Indigenous Peoples whose
footsteps have marked these territories on which peoples of the world
now gather.

Library and Archives Canada Cataloguing in Publication

Title: Whiny baby / Julie Paul.

Names: Paul, Julie, 1969- author.

Series: Hugh MacLennan poetry series.

Description: Series statement: The Hugh MacLennan poetry series

Identifiers: Canadiana (print) 20230572537 | Canadiana (ebook)
20230572553 | ISBN 9780228020745 (softcover) |
ISBN 9780228020752 (PDF) | ISBN 9780228020769 (ePUB)

Subjects: LCGFT: Poetry.

Classification: LCC PS8631.A8498 W45 2024 | DDC C811/.6—dc23

This book was typeset by Marquis Interscript in 9.5/12 Sabon.

For my writing allies

CONTENTS

Contents

Contents

BIRDING AT NIGHT

In the tiny meadow behind the school
I lay on grass so soft it felt like
the breast of a songbird.
Spring wildflowers spoke to me:
hepatica called in powdered tones,
bloodroot whistled and sang scat,
violets spoke in rhyming couplets,
fresh maple leaves whispered sibilant S's.
What lived there beyond what I could see?
I'd been nowhere special
but knew the names of places to visit:
Italy, New York, Australia, Mexico, Timbuktu.
I was afraid of space, and got lost in malls
but Paris, watch out.
Who knew the best way to leave?
I felt my dead Mama's hand in mine as I lay there
staring at the new leaves above.
Something like wind began to call.
I walked further
until I found a young girl, waiting in the woods.
It was me, walking.
It was me, waiting.

Mama, my maternal grandma, always said

Don't be bold

which meant

Don't be rude

which meant
speaking
my mind or feelings,

so I clamped my mouth right up

tight as my Catholic thighs

years before I knew
that was the boldest place
from which to speak.

One grandma used God,
the other Zest,

and they both worked wonders
to keep me clean enough

to hold their love
and my seat in heaven,

a chair that was never guaranteed
to still be there
when the music stopped.

MEA CULPA: CEDAR GROVE
CASTLE CONFITEOR

We wore our hair in crown braids
and although your name was a pretty one
I called you Elizabeth, Mary, whatever I wanted.

In our make-believe castle behind my house
– cedar trees circling an old barn's foundation –
I would judge and decree from an overturned washtub,
banish feckless siblings to the backyard sandbox,
but keep you, my friend, close by my side.

Imagined subjects bowed and praised
our rule – beneficent but firm –
waited for ceremony,
lifted their hands to our skirts.

One illumined day – or was it every day? –
I was blessed by the frisson of sudden truth:
I was more priest than queen,
more god than royalty,
more anything than you.

I ordered you to gather fallen boughs,
their crumbling filigree,
then sprinkled their rust upon your forehead
and demanded not only fealty but sorrow.

What choice did you give me?

You were younger than me by a year, wore
misshapen handmade sweaters;
holey cable tights wormed up your legs.
You ate scabby apples right down to the stem.

My belted white nightgown, ruffled, flowing,
stood in as a royal gown, and in case you forgot:
it proclaimed *Angel* in gold script above the heart.

TWISTER

Dalhousie Lake, Summer 1981

Remember the morning air,
mostly water, pressing
its million fingerprints against our skin

and how we erased its touch in the lake
floating starfish, dead mans,
the sky gathering secret troops

at the lake's western head,
clouds unnoticed until their faint rumble
reminded us of our hunger.

Remember casually emerging,
checking feet for leeches,
wrapping in breeze-stiffened towels

as the first colossal drops
and petrichor
and the thundering army advanced,

and how the screen door slapped behind us
as we shrieked into the cottage, still dripping wet
yet desperate to shelter from the rain.

Remember how we stood at the windows and watched
the weather approach, not a marching wall
of soldiers as it usually seemed

but a cloud like a wasp's nest
advancing and then suddenly upon us, a roar
and one, two, three,

the trees in the neighbour's yard fell like pins
while a crash from our porch resounded,
the BBQ toppled and lawn chairs flew

and we rushed, as toddler screamed,
baby cried, and windows blew open,
to huddle as one behind bedroom doors.

Remember dishes and sandwiches flying
from the table, and all of us together, in the face of it,
never as close except for Sears portraits, a family of six

in the path of a twister – and then just as quick,
it was over, it had moved on, away from us, the air as clear
as relief as we separated safely back into ourselves.

BEFORE THE DIVORCE

Empress Hotel, Victoria, BC

Here is a coast; here is a harbour;
and here is the ivy-costumed hotel
built on a filled-in swamp –
what could possibly go wrong?
Here is where your parents celebrate
their twenty-fifth anniversary
in one small, haunted room that faces the sunset,
one last act for the children who saved to pay for it.
From their window they offer brave faces and advice
to you, standing on the lawn below: the golden boy
and his three big sisters, you in charge for the night.
You wave up at them, send reassurances of your survival
before gallivanting to the causeway
and its souvenir hawkers,
its vendors of mirth. You leave them up there,
trapped like a portrait in the window frame,
and you, the four reasons they've stayed together,
walk among the fancy boats with waffle cones,
counting seals in the oily harbour.

AFTER LOSING HIS FATHER,
AND THEN HIS BROTHER

The tradition began. Every Sunday night,
my young father took his shirts next door
to his mother, who ironed them
for a dollar a piece.

The money was not the point.
Neither was the ironing
although the shirts needed pressing
for the work week ahead.

In Nana's practiced hand,
on her silver-skinned board,
the iron hissed and spit like a demon
and didn't miss a single thread.

She always said she loved the job,
but of course it was my father she loved,
and having a way to reach him
from her island of loss,

which was his island too:
they were calling from different shores
across the same dark waters
to one another

and answering
with wrinkled shirts,
a problem she could solve
before the evening news.

18 February 2018

We gathered in Clydesville
and walked across the solid river
to go up the hill and then down again.
A dozen of us created a path through fresh snow
between the birches and the pines
just for the beauty of it, because
we could, because we wanted
to bathe in the glittering winter light.
And we took turns on the snow
machines, on paths through the frozen marshes
and behind the houses, and we skated
on the rink my uncle had made on the Clyde,
and pulled the little kids in sleighs, and watched
our words and laughter hang in the air like prayers.
We drank hot chocolate, beer, whatever
we needed – I mean, we needed Nana
and she was gone – but with every sip
we drank to her, the way we did with maple whisky
that first night in her house without her,
a whole bottle gone in one toast:
there were that many of us in the house and it still felt empty.
The wake, the funeral, the burial, the reception –
all of those memories feel like pressed leaves,
a cut-off braid curled in a jewellery box,
a hand-embroidered tablecloth, a pinned butterfly.
But that day on the river? It glows like a yellow bird's breast,
burns in the throat like whisky,
a pleasure-pain inflicted by the animal that is love,
the wild thrash of its radiant heart.

GRAVITY DOESN'T SEEM
AS STRONG NOW

Did I tell you
she was good?
What I mean is that
she was good
in the way
the world most needs.
By world
I mostly mean
the small planet
of our family,
its solid core
turned to vapour.

The dress she wore to your wedding
is not the same dress she was buried in.
One was the colour of a Bohemian waxwing,
the other an eastern bluebird.
You're not crying; there's sleep in your eyes,
or is it the smoke, the pollen, your lack of self-restraint?
The land of grief has you cowbirded,
an egg abandoned in the nest of another species
that will, in turn, eventually do the same to her own.
Who's writing this song? A woman in the dark,
listening to a conversation between two barred owls.
What is longing?
Hands reaching like wings around nothing that can be held.
The woman = you. The woman = anyone.
The owls ask the same question, back and forth:
Hoo-hoo, hoo-hoo, hoo-hoo hoo-hoooooah.
The answer is a hard apple, swallowed whole.
No one cooks for you.

ENDEMIC

WHINY BABY

I live on the easiest coast of all,
where the air's sea-scoured
and the drifts are made mostly from blossoms,
and I have the temerity to say
I don't truly feel at home.

Oh yay, that old chestnut of a quest.
I would bore myself to death if I wasn't so stubborn.

But what if I've been seeking a singular source
when the opposite is true
and I could find a sense of home everywhere?

Maybe it is only, always, plural and global –
but can my ego be so large, to need a home that big?

Or maybe my life's pursuit is simply to feel comfortable
in the world itself, as a temporary resident
or visitor or caretaker, call it what you will.
None of us will last this whole thing out.

I read today that there are places on Earth
where gravity is stronger, and they aren't on Vancouver Island,
but I can't blame that for my willingness to leave.

I think the wanderlust's from another source,
a graininess afflicting my blood
when in one place too long,
a sedimentation of sorts
when all cheese turns to chalk
and the sun isn't shining right and the wind
makes my hair part on the side that gives me a headache
and I become a whiny baby again, difficult to soothe.

I don't believe in sticking to blooming where you're planted,
but if planted, yes, by all means, flower away.
Wildflowers tuck themselves into hollows and grooves,
but they also stand tall in the high spots too, wind-bobbed
and valiant.

Never mind the whining.
The air smells freshly showered.
As it turns out, there is so much I can complain about
and even more to love.

I am chomping / champing at the bit,
straining against my harness, again.

I both fear horses and revere them;
it's the same with wolves and the sea.

These familiar streets don't offer much
beyond the mildest of changes / non-changes,
and me noting them like an elder person
which isn't far off

Chomping / champing / championing / churlish

It isn't interiors that push or pull me so much
as milieu, environs, locale –

Why so much French?
It's *sans surprise*.
Montreal's whispering in my ear:
Oui oui. Viens ici.

But what does it want me for?
I'm just another greying lady
in a Bench vest
sweating behind her reading glasses
wishing for anything else good
beyond the obvious good I'm in.

There's a wolf at the door
that looks exactly like me.

HERE IS WHERE?

View Royal, BC

Here is where I walk beneath the alders and their gold
    jewellery and say, oh, wow.

Here is where I look out at the island I have never set
    foot on
but to which my husband swam during the heat dome
    and think, you again.

Here is where I answer the phone and hear my daughter's
    laughter from the other side
of the country, accordion and café murmurs in the
    background. There, my heart.

Here is where I look down and snap photos of kelp
    and shells and sand and say nothing.

Here is where I stand, mute, waiting for something else
    to speak.

And when it does, it is the small clear voice inside me,
    saying yes, this, and also something more, please.

It is the other me again, wanting – no big ask – a second
    life alongside this one.
Not because this one needs replacing, but because
    it doesn't.

DRIVING DOWN FAITHFUL STREET

Victoria, BC

I meet numerous stop signs
while the cross streets
are all   go   go   go

       this is not a metaphor

I could turn down
     or up
any number of avenues

head north, out of town

or south, straight into the sea

but instead

I cruise along Faithful
listening to night jazz

dreaming of escaping
this city, mild as a house mouse
or husband
or cheddar
or me.

You river city, you island nation,
you ration your warmth, softness, common sense,
spew water in streets and metro stations
from broken pipes as ancient and immense
as your charm. There's no other location
quite like yours to make both embrace and wall
from two tongues, no better source of elation
for the young who come to shake off boredom,
or the once-young who yearn to turn back time.
You've ensnared my daughter with your sublime
façades, song, cuisine from every kingdom –
she hated you at ten, fresh from the west,
but says her home is now your fickle breast.
Can you guess? I'm afflicted, like the rest.

CRIDGEON

Montreal, QC

> Winter lives under a pigeon's wing, a dead wing with
> damp feathers.
>
> "Paris, 7 a.m.," Elizabeth Bishop

Winter lives everywhere here, true, non-negotiable winter,
and my jade scarf, a flimsy coastal fashion piece not
meant for barricading ears and face, still looks beautiful
next to my wind-burnt cheeks. Colour, beauty, food,
music, language, visits to my only daughter: ways the city
offers itself to me. Other ways: the buildings make tunnels
for the wind to run up and down. The snow comes gusting
in through any crack, any gap in the armour, but it also
collects like wet stars in our hair. The truth of the city
comes in mad kisses to my toes, blistered from new snow
boots, and in the static in my flattened hair from hats and
forced furnace air. It comes in the buoyancy in my heart
and bones and spirit at witnessing my daughter in love,
adulting, and at myself, alone and diving back into history,
looking for my old self around every corner from when
I lived here long ago. What is the source of all joy and
grief and longing except the struggle to love as best as
possible what's right in front of you? Even the cold. Even
the pre-emptive sadness at having to leave tomorrow.
And so the black pigeon we see dragging its wing
as it pecks at salt and ice is only a source of interest.
A *cridgeon*, we name it. A crow / pigeon mix, not a
metaphor, not today.

I walk the long narrow streets of Le Plateau-Mont-Royal,
alongside row houses, flat-roofed, jewel-toned, dripping
with ivy and wrought iron, angles no longer true. I find
my way down alleys no longer passable except by bike
or foot or paw. These streets hold cardinals welcoming
spring, neighbours laughing, late voters at the polling
station arguing with officials for their right to cast their
ballot, my daughter's puppy, broken sticks in her gentle
mouth, an opera singer in a tuxedo with his clown-suited
dog by the fountain, where the statue of another old
conqueror holds a giant, empty bottle of beer.

Mom's wedding china
on my daughter's table
three thousand miles from home.

In the waiting room
I tell you I feel like Miss America.
I've got both eyes, rosy cheeks, a fresh haircut,
the strap of my raw silk purse across my chest. A sash.
We walked here, hand in hand,
through autumn leaves.

My wonky boob notwithstanding,
still blue from dye to find the node they took
and prone to nervy pain around the nipple,
I'm good as gold.
Spot's all gone, surgeon says.
Nothing left in there at all.

The oncologist calls it
a well-behaved tumour,
but I can claim no sway.
It's been deposited into the tissue bank,
slices of me sealed and filed for future use,
future study, future girls. In the future,
will I take credit if I remain cancer-free?
Sink with guilt and shame if I don't?

I'm throwing everything at it
except drugs or zaps, politely
trading standards of care for grape skins,
berries, tinctures, tennis, paint.

I didn't know you were a gambler,
you say on our walk back home.
Same here, I reply. But either way's a risk.

I lift my head high, hear the roar of a crowd,
sashay past a row of judges.
Or are they only the Garry oaks
along the sidewalk, nodding, applauding?

ENDEMIC

The natural history of this archipelago is very remarkable:
it seems to be a little world within itself.

Charles Darwin

And here we are. Today's yearning
involves teleportation to Ecuador,
among the animals that live nowhere else.
Galapagos: even the word is a journey.
My mouth wants to chew upon its caramel syllables,
my brain hungers for a holiday
where I say *platypus* every day.
Instead, I am struggling to breathe on this mildewed coast,
chest tightening as we head into another Covid winter
after a summer of smoky skies – choking not from disease
but from pre-emptive anxiety, abraded privilege,
stretched awareness, exhaustion. Will any of us
ever be the same? Do I want to know the answer?
The Before Times glow in my like head
like blue-footed boobies and lava gulls,
like diving marine iguanas and Sally Lightfoot crabs
on black sand. Those days were always endangered species –
I just didn't want to admit it. And now, I'm no better.
I'm still imagining that *the little world within itself*
also known as this one hot mess we call home –
from seahorses to five-hundred-pound tortoises –
will be saved by a superhero who'll do more than I do,
sitting around hoping for a mass miracle
that only a God I don't believe in could provide.

You want to let me go, but you keep scrolling
and listening to the radio.
Is it lethargy or habit or love, keeping you in chains?

To resist me takes muscle, but you're not the violent type.
Put up your dukes, though.
Gimme all you got.

Shove the newspaper in the bin, unread.
Your thin carapace won't keep
the horrors from seeping in.

It's likely that the sponge holds water,
not vinegar or virus,
but Jesus and I have tainted your outlook.

Stick a hashtag in front of an eggplant or peach
and you're advertising erections or buttocks.
Use frequently, as you see fit.

Your dear brain has a fondness for bootlegging
the day's worries into the darkness, multiplying them tenfold.
Wanna know who profits? Hint: it isn't you.

When dream frights make you peripatetic,
you turn to lavender, baths, counted breaths.
Eggplant and/or peaches are more likely to work (see above).

Sometimes you just need a paperback escape hatch.
Try it. Sink completely into a story
where the hero gets away.

Everyone tells you to move on, release me, surrender to life.
Listen: I'm not leaving you. I adore you.
I've got your back until the day you die.

AUTOPHAGY

From soft thing to soft thing
I devour the world,
as if the gods won't bring
another, as if these squirrelled-
away bits of nutrition,
these particular solutions for hunger,
will be the last ingestion
this machine will ever plunder.
I'm both right and very wrong –
the cycles turn and burn and turn,
the plants and stories rise from death anon.
Yet, always, I'm still hungry. I yearn.
Nothing is immune from my hunter's appetite.
No one, not even me, is ever safely out of sight.

In this morning's dream
there is a lot of lake
and a child, my friend's, who is a lot,
not doing what we want,
and a bit of bribery
and a discovery:
two rocks stuck together,
a mollusk, the glue,
a sadness at the boy
not being amazed,
wanting YouTube instead
and a bag of marshmallows –
sticky white slugs when wet.

Then there's me in an elevator, alone,
holding the door for a man
who gets up close to me
and says I'm lucky
I'm not a baby,
he likes them young,
shows me something with his fingers
I can never unsee:
another close call
that even in a dream
feels like assault all the same.

I want to go back to sleep,
return to the other night's dream
of a giant cougar in my yard
from which I woke with a start
as much from awe as fear;
a better beast to carry
through the coming day,
that ochre fur,
those familiar eyes.

THE SOURCE OF THE SINGING

We longed to find the source of the singing but our
legs were broken. Well, not broken, but unusable,
untrustworthy. In fact they were fine, our legs, but we'd
forgotten how to walk and there was no one left to lead
the way. Did we want a leader? We thought of other
leaders, how they'd taken their people to glory and/or
graves and we decided it wasn't worth the risk. But the
singing – the melody seeped through the cracks in the wall
like the scent of a lemon tart. The voices harmonized as if
the wind and sea, sky and light, had joined forces to take
us down. We felt a deep twitch in our hamstrings. Our toes
grabbed at the dirt. Who dared to make such a joyful noise,
we whispered, our vocal cords long turned to rust. We
longed to find the source of sound. The urge to move grew
louder within us, swelled to mirror the choral crescendo
that haunted us. But instead we sat with our backs against
the wall and let the music ruin us, note by note.

GRIEF DUPLEX

Hornby Island, BC

In memory of J.G.

I watch the pond like it's theatre,
a mid-week spot-lit matinee

as I mourn, still, and again,
a friend murdered one year ago.

A year ago the air was half smoke
as wildfires devoured whole towns,

towns first maimed by virus, then eaten by flames
that sent smoke across the country.

Across the country my daughter sings in bars
where my friend once made art on beer coasters

while I coast and swim through a late summer heat wave,
sun hot as fresh grief on my skin.

Murderer still at large, my grief renewed,
I watch the pond's theatrics until night snuffs out the sun.

HOUSEHOLD HAUNTING, OR QUESTIONS
ABOUT MY ANXIETY

The sad seamstress who stays with us this month
assures me she'll be leaving soon.
Do ghosts pack their own suitcases?
If asked at the checkpoint, could she honestly say
she packed it herself and then be allowed
to pass through to the other side?
What if she's stolen a child from here,
catatonic over leaving?
What if the case is filled with poison raspberry gumdrops?
What if it holds shards of glass, reflecting our blue-grey sky?
Did she even sew a stitch while in our generous home?
I wanted to give her everything broken,
my holey cashmere, my rotten tooth,
my empty heart, my tangled chains, this brain,
all of it, but she never seemed receptive to my woes,
possibly distracted by the amorphous place
she'd landed, unable to help after all.
And perhaps – perhaps she has no plans
for leaving, after all. Maybe the only way
to get rid of her is to pack my own suitcase too,
squeeze every bone and sorrow inside,
take us both to the border
and make them let us through.
Yes. Travelling together, I'll say.
Nothing to declare.

I attend this event with a friend;
four poets on a panel dive deep
into long form poetry as a way
to more fully share their histories:
invisibility, negation, assault, torture.

        The focus is on taking up space
        as female / genderqueer / deaf
        and showing the work in long poems,
        asking questions and giving enough space
        to mull and meander to a possible answer.
        The audience gasps, laughs, cries, together.

A young man walks in, late,
during Sumita Chakraborty's long poem
about family violence. A hundred questions
drown out all her words.

        Does he have a gun?
        Does he know her?
        Is he the brother in the poem?
        Did her voice change
        when he sat right in front of her
        second row back?

My thoughts won't stop.
I scan the room for exits, security,
other people who are on high alert like me.
My friend seems unfazed.
She takes notes on the poem,
as I was doing, a moment ago.

       No one checked our bags coming in,
       no pat downs, no detectors of any sort,
       all we got was an email after registration
       about the conference's weapons policy
       – not allowed.

I laughed when I read that,
then shook my Canadian head in dismay,
then forgot about it until now.

       Is a poet made from danger
       in danger? Is a woman telling the truth
       dangerous, or is it dangerous to simply be alive
       in America, caught in the crossfire
       of an ordinary day?

We are all vulnerable here.
No skin a match for metal.
After three years
of fearing the very air,
shoulders are finally settling,
until someone sneezes.

I look at the crowd, take a quick count:
less than 5 per cent are identifiable as male.
Does that make this group safer
or simply a bigger target?

The man sits down and stays there,
witnesses along with the rest of us
how pain and violence
shared in the lines of a poem
can become weapons to fight future
pain and violence, or at least offer
a way to make us feel less alone.

Later the same day
during the keynote presentation,
we stay at home in our pyjamas
and tune into the live stream on our phones,
eating cheese and chocolate,
the right answer to the problem
of how to end this long day well.

WHAT HUMANS DO

In memory of V.B. and L.A.

You must have biscuits with your coffee and you must call them
biscuits. You lived in Montreal once, not jolly old England, so
you have to say it like this: *bee-squee*. Although the city you are
in has been called by many a "Little England," you are drinking
dark coffee, not tea. If you blot out the last two letters of this
city's name you get a winner. Or, the name of your friend's dad
who was listening to Daniel Lanois on his death bed, watching
Jeopardy! and shouting out the answers five days before the
cancer won. This morning, Daniel's song "Babette" came on the
CBC and your daughter said, hey, they're singing in Franglais.
After she got dropped off at school, late, because she went to the
opera last night, you ran through the park listening to Björk and
smelling heliotrope, candy for the nasal cells. You are alive and
all your parts are working. The grounds of your coffee swirl like
smoke in the last half-inch of creamy goodness. You said inch,
you Little Brit. It's still a remarkable day on earth.

GREENER GRASS MASH-UP

Below my personal suspension
bridge   of disbelief
lives a troll who mistakes my footprints
for those of scared ruminants

despite their mechanical precision

tok   tok   tok   tok

and now he's hungry, thinking goats

but it's just me and my high heels talking
since I no longer rely on blocks or the phone book
to bring me up to table height.

Yes, I'm short
and no one lets me forget –
except the temporarily tiny

Oh, but I was a God
until my daughter sprouted skyward!
                    Wait, was that the phone?
                    I should call her. She might need me.

Maybe I should hang out exclusively
with toddlers,
            preferably ones who talk
in sugar-coated cereal voices

Snap! Crackle! Pop!

I do not need high heels
nor do I complain when these youngsters want

Up!   Up!   Up!   Up!

Who doesn't long for altitude
before it's replaced by attitude
and eventually decrepitude
and then, only blended food?

Toddler Trolls Rule the World!
                    Hang on, I should thaw meat for dinner.

*

My own personal troll
            (inner child
            demon critic
            whiny baby)
stopped maturing when
it was most convenient for him,
eternally stuck in a puddle-jumping phase.

It's NOT A PHASE, he screams, mud
spraying the curtains (at least he's potty-trained –
small mercies – nothing worse than a diapered troll
    beneath the bridge).

What's the word on the street, these days,
about bypassing trolls?
No words. Only pictures,
worth so much more, or so they say, LOLZ!
                    Is this light good for a selfie?

Although this fixation with the perfect ratio
of followers to following on Instagram
begs for meta-analysis, it seems I am
still going to document every step and share,
because caring is sharing!

No one knows the perfect recipe for living
this thing out. Is it aging in place?
Sounds statuesque
and statues can't cross bridges –

Anyway, I'm going across that bridge,
ignoring what lies beneath
                              Unless there are dishes to do?

*

Troll likes to sing Christmas carols, jingles;
he bites his thumbs   bites me
still   I love him

but there's no denying
I can get a lot more done
when he naps.

Without Troll it's just a bridge over
untroubled waters,
just a span
Attention!
over a troll-shaped space

Snapchat *that*, why dontcha!
Serenity now!

He keeps me jumping and I am not a jumper
(nor a sweater)   (nor a bunny hug)

I bet he'll grow up to be a hockey player with playoff hair
I bet he'll ignore my texts
I bet he'll drink himself stupid
I bet he'll marry for love
                    and I am not a betting woman

See what he does to me? Instead of creating
I ruminate, speculate, pontificate
and now I'm late, very late –

Mama, Troll cries.

Up?   Up?   Up?   Up?
                                        Ummm, is that cake?

Some days I simply live for the promise of cake.

Troll, are you listening?
We can both agree on this one.

Hear the glass lid settle on the counter – hats off!
Cake is coming, clangs the clear bell!

Cake is scrumptious!
Troll is silent

Cake is gone but for the smears
There but for the –

I thank thee, day, for this most amazing cake,
and each farmer, sugar cane harvester, each bead
of sweat in the cinnamon peeler's eye, each egg
come out the vent –
cloaca, if you prefer –

which sounds a lot like *cluck*, although does a hen
really make that sound? Mexican roosters say *quiquiriquí*
but it's all poppycock to me

(Now that's a snack my troll would dig.
Oh, bring back, bring back,
oh bring back the Seventies to me, to me ...)
                                        Ooh, popcorn!

*

All the collared girls go
Doot de doot, doot, doot de doot, doot
and pass me on the bridge carrying Mason jars
of ten dollar juice
to their hot yoga change rooms
seeking bliss and/or thigh gaps
even though the latest word – never the last –
is that a chubby upper leg can save your heart.

My fist makes a most satisfying thwick
against my thigh
thick   thigh   thwick   thwick

A bounce, a firmness:
Who dares to walk upon my bridge?

I am not my footsteps, nor my patella,
femur, rib, or sternum
nor adipose tissue –

Sorry, Troll. It's only me.
                        God, do I need a manicure.

*

The union of bones,
we most often call a joint
but why not the Latinate *articulation*?

My lifelong quest: how to best articulate?
To write as if every sentence
is a matchmaker, bringing lovers together –
or at least a word or two.

No one is twisting any Gruff's arm
to go eat daisies and clover and sweet grass
but I can hear that meadow singing its promises –
a sweet harmonic blend that squeezes my arm
and pulls, pleading

Come   come   come   COME!

If I should ever see the world
in a grain of fentanyl
or from outer space
would I even want to return
to this plainer kind of bliss?
Those who know say
No.

                                  I think I hear the kettle.

*

Maybe I need company to cross!
Come with me, then, Gruffly,
across this old wooden bridge
trip trap   or   stomp stomp
if that's how
you   do   you.

Ignore what's beneath,
eyes front, and
Courage! Godspeed! Lift your little feet.
                    Wait, Downton Abbey, *season five?*

I'm talking words here, but if this isn't about art
for you
then substitute whatever it is that lights you up –
whatever fills the blank after retirement

If you are afraid of the blank where "work" once was
then may I suggest:
pretty much anything?

Because:

People
Die
All
The
Time
in the months just after the golden handshake –
system shutdown, no system restore

All that non-Beyoncé grinding, and for what?

Do you dare, do you dare
to cross that bridge
when you come to it
when it comes down to it
when it becomes up to you
what will you do –

Trip trap?   March on?

Long have I lived as if there will be no retirement,
contrary to popular wisdom or science on life spans,
    etcetera
no nest egg or home building itself into cash,
no folks about to bequeath
a fortune, no buried treasure, heirloom jewellery,
stocks, bonds, barrels of oil in the backyard –

Nothing as far as my eye can see
to save my later years

But maybe? Troll asks. A real job? A pension?

No.
I'm crossing.

                              I smell burning toast.

*

I have set dates for pounds lost
but somehow hunger overrides
the future fit potential
of every dress

and every future is only a potential
the way energy sits in a piece of wood
until burned   if burned
    Am I worth more now or when?

A poem is no RRSP
but how will l live if not by heaving words,
stacking syllables like bricks of peat –

Troll, am I boring you?

Muse   muse   snooze   snooze

Are we done yet? he asks.

And I say   again   No.
But you can go to sleep.

                    I miss the smell of my daughter's head.

*

Perhaps my favourite time of day
is five after nine, on either end:

Day's gently begun   or
day's nearly done.

My babe arrived at nine a.m. exactly
so at five past I was high on hormones,
oblivious of the job yet to come

Placenta – what?
Are you serious?

push   push   push   push

Again? No thanks. Been there, done that, thank you very
      much!

And what's this tiny wet head wanting?
Oh, only me.

I bet she'll be an aristocrat
I bet she'll be first at bat
I bet she'll dress the cat in drag
And I am not a betting –

MAMA!

Troll, go to sleep,
you're interrupting my pronouncements,
some already true.

The self-aware must deliver bulletins
to the masses awaiting royal velvet words:

To thine own self be
truly
ridiculous.
Isn't it good to laugh?

*

Velvet were our childhood jumpers
over white collared blouses at Mass

And all the collared girls – sisters, three –
said   Amen   Amen   Amen
to the thin body of Christ in our hands

Lord, not worthy, blah blah, I get it,
but say the word, won't you?
I'd like to get home to Disney
or a ski in the woods.

In that rural childhood we drank water
from a goatskin wine pouch on the ski trails,
its bladdery pagan goodness
so squeezable, our mouths dry with exertion
from sidestepping or herringboning up the hills,
pushing fast on the flats if the snow was right
or slogging through feet of it

red balloon cheeks
hands hot in our mittens
until they came off for the Gorp
'good ol' raisins and peanuts' –

God bless the late twentieth century.

*

Holy Moses. Perhaps I am not even a goat.

What if I'm a bird instead
and can simply fly over the need for a bridge altogether?

I need to know my species, y'all!
Then I can get on with it, whatever this is.
The secret to success is –

Troll, no need for rousing.

My identities contain multitudes.
The church bell sounds hoarse today.

*

One teenage day sewn into memory:
Carmanah Valley on a Sunday morning
and my aunt made me leave to go to church.

I don't know if she was more afraid
of wolves or God –
My, what big teeth you have!

But touching the river in that northern rainforest
was a cold clear sacrament
and I put my face in and drank
before I trudged back up the trail to get me
to an acceptable worship space:

Glory be to God for dappled light on the rental car.
                    My mouth is watering.

*

What's your poison? Cake?
Or the grassy knoll so sweet?

Every campaign to get my attention / money
hinges on the concept that a product
is the bridge between lack and bliss

buy   buy   buy   buy

and save my soul
or at least a couple of bucks.

But of course there are trolls under every bridge!
My, what big wallets you have!

I, too, am American Eagle
Outfitters.
        BOGO sale ends tonight!

*

I should say something here
about my research on the fad of structures,

how post-war preference for meat on bones
birthed brewer's yeast advertisements, guaranteed to fatten
even the skinniest into curving bombshells

until bones became all the rage
ribs a counting tool
thigh gap   the most coveted space

absence defines
the lack thereof
the best waist   fits inside a ring
made by a man's joined hands

and girls in every season
walk runways   tightropes   lines
walk the walk   the talk
in their heads   a dark static
of sniggers and jeers and admonishments
and also in the mix   a plaintive cry:
                    I'm hungry. Need to eat.

Cake?

*

The bones in my hands have been talking
– articulating –
and man, do they want a holiday. Greener grass?

I shall photograph my resting hand
and post it with the caption: "grateful."
Or less sappy, "working towards fifty years of service"
or "Can I get a witness?"   or "slow clap for this
   clapper."

On weaker days
I wonder if I should just stay here, Troll and me.

Day's weak? Days, weeks, months, sometimes

even though I am hungry
even though I am lonely
even though all that's left on this side
is a bunch of dead weeds and burdock wanting my fur,
even if burrs were the inspiration behind Velcro

Troll, you want to win, don't you?
                                        Everyone loves a winner!

Maybe I should do it: shop
my feelings away
or eat them
or sex them up instead

But isn't it quiet on the other side?
Does the silence wait for me?

I have heard the words singing, each to each –

What words?
Best words.   Bad words.   Any words.

Anything as long as it's sweet.

*

Pretty please, can we keep walking?

When please becomes pretty
it gets more dates
but what's under that fascinator?
Can please make a funny? Can please
make a valid argument?

So, this is a praise poem.

Not rage, rage against the –
but praise, praise against the –

Despite people eating animal brains
and leftovers from garbage cans
isn't it a lovely day?
Wait, let me check the weather app.

No, Troll, I will not adjust myself
Do not adjust your set
The revolution will not be PVR'd
The revolution because of the revulsion and etc. etc.
The lies come out
like ribbon candy

Oh. That's not candy.

Can this still be a praise poem
despite changes in administration,
muzzles and shock collars for everyone?

*

Ain't no hole in the oh-zone
big enough to drive a car through
but that most famous drive-thru tree in California
Pioneer Cabin Tree
recently died,
a winter storm to blame and not the hole –
                    giant sequoia, how are ya now?

Just as happy as the dance-floor beauty
The Discovery Tree
twenty-four-foot diameter that took twenty-two days to kill?

No mention of how long to polish it
into a dance floor for forty people
or make a saloon and bowling alley
over its fallen trunk.

(God, is there anything better than driving your car
through something? Thrills every second.
See: head in a lion's mouth
See: hanging off the CN tower
See: eating Japanese pufferfish.)

Wait, isn't this what a Gruff might do,
once she/me crosses that bridge?
Can she be trusted to simply create good things?
I might manifest my destiny all over you
so hard ...

Maybe Troll is the one to watch –
gatekeeper extraordinaire.
Ones to watch under thirty!
The brave and talented rising stars!

*

Could this become a pastoral instead?
No.
I turn from nature poems as if commanded
to eat quinoa in everything.

I love "Nature," though,
and who better than a "poet"
to illuminate the "impermanence,"
the "beauty and ruin"

if these words are not forbidden yet?

The eye,
the i –

    It's personal,
cellular.

         Have you seen my phone?

But I believe in angels
and art deco and avocado toast
and all the other amazing *A* words –
you have no idea the wealth in every letter.

That's what I'm talking about –
I've cut no thousand-year trees down
to send to England or dance upon their bones

With every smug sip from my fox mug I can see
the adorable face peek more from beneath the edge
of my wondrous latte, containing
no dead songbirds, slavery, sweat, or shite –
Isn't *S* a naughty letter today?
I'm boycotting it entirely.

Instead I will continue "borrowing" from those Gruffs
who've already crossed, even ABBA.

I believe in angles!
I believe in aardvarks
I believe in absolutes:

Jail to those who high-grade the trail mix
Jail to those offended by pussy hats
(not merkins, I don't mean merkins, I never mean
    merkins)

How do I know what I meme until I meme what I say?
I am slow to take
exception and make my taking slow,
learn by going where I should not go.
    I think I'm thirsty.

Shall I compare thee to a summer sale on beer?
Thou art cheaper and more temporary.

*

In the good dream the gunmen don't see me
but I see them shooting others
and can do nothing about it but hide.

In the bad dream –
Who has time for bad dreams? This is a praise ...

I shall wear my privilege and walk upon
the fallen ears from the Colonel's table
unless you can tell me who to trust?

It is not myself (bird, goat, what?)
it is not the government

It might be cake, if someone dares
to bake a tiny hammer into it

                              Did you say cake again?

Trip trap goes the little hammer
fixing the bridge to keep trolls out of sight
and the way clear.

Do you follow me,
Dog / Dawg?

Unfollow me
if I do offend.

This is still not the end.

*

My daughter wrote a song at three
about her backpack   and the last lines went like this:
"That is the wend of the song
and   I a-am   always   done."

58

I proceed, wending my way, mistakes
coming from mouths as poetic oopses
occasionally caught on film
or paper
or bits of bytes
for future weddings or memorials.

Luck has everything to do
with what side of the coin sees the light.

She also used to ask
for reasons lost to history: *Are you shy or lucky?*

Well, which one is it?
Do I dare to cross that bridge
when I come to the path
not taken   seriously
this has got to   stop   in the name of
love   me   tender

(Insert rhyming couplet):

Dear Troll, in the end, we've only got each other
but please, please don't eat my bigger brother ...
                              My profile pic is ancient.
                              Time for an update!

I grow old, I grow cold,
when the Facebook app won't load.

God, please, just let me   finally   trip trap
over the bridge

even if the only thing I create
is the noise of feet on boards

or a GIF of the breeze riffling clover
in silent   lyrical   ways.

Once I'm in range again,
someone   somewhere
will save me
by liking what I post
from the other side.
What's the wifi password again?

One word, all lower case: trollwins.

TODAY, AT LEAST

TELOMERE REPAIR,
FIRST PANDEMIC SPRING

in the oak meadow   I can feel   my telomeres
not shrinking for a change   but plumping up a little even
like long balloons   with a little water in them
and the breeze   gives high fives
the grass   encourages my calves
this moment   is not optional   extra   or frivolous
it is   instead of   the grocery store
even though we are   out of fruit
and I am nourished   by the ladybug
the vetch   the camas   even the Scotch broom
that blares its yellow music   into the native species' faces
my feet are bare   the sun leans against my back
like a friend
if we could have friends   this close
I press against it   and longer grow the telomeres
I have no choice   but to try and save myself
like I save seeds
imagining future gardens   growing   in future springs
take another breath   I tell myself
high five   says the breeze again
I lean against the sun   and watch a vulture
assess the situation   and then fly east
nothing here   just yet   to see.

that gave me nightmares
or maybe it was the giant hole
in the logic of importing butter
from New Zealand
or the giant hole in the ozone –
wait, isn't that healing? Didn't we do
one thing right? I don't miss hairspray.
Or maybe it was the giant gap
between me and the suffering
and yet I am still suffering,
still count myself among them,
paper cuts versus daggers,
but I woke up dreaming of three sick children
and me sure I'd gotten the virus from them
as I cleaned up their puke and fed them
from what I could find in their messy home
and I can't shake the kids from my awareness
all the kids, all hurting
more because of lockdowns
more because of suffering
more because hurting people hurt more people
and it hits me that karma is just another word for tough luck
another way to wash one's hands of helping
but what can I do? I'm sitting in a meadow of wildflowers
writing this on my new-model phone
with organic sunscreen on my face
and no one trying to make me suffer
just because they're suffering,
although I'm pretty good at doing that to myself
but that's small potatoes
baby ones

that would taste divine smothered in butter
from grass-fed cows
flown here from a country that got the pandemic right
and is led by a brilliant woman.
I also dreamt of gifts and winning money
that I would likely spend on myself
the way I bought a $200 sweater last month
the exact colour of a distant sky   oh
there is likely little hope for me
I can turn the radio off when the annoying songs come on
and although they haunt me for the rest of the day
if this is all the haunting that today offers up
then I can only call it lucky
although I also mean ridiculous
and unfair.
I just need someone to tell me what to do and I'll do it
but even before I tap out these words
I know they're a pretty little lie.

TODAY, AT LEAST

The light coming in
and the light going out
are the same colour.

And not least of all
I have today   and this body

the same thick wrists
I had at ten

the same eyes that can spot a spelling mistake
or a blue jay from a hundred feet away

the same ears that sought quiet nooks
behind the sawmill,
not for groping or necking, same neck

but for filling up with birdsong
and non-songs
of to-dos and sister cries

the same thighs that still touch each other
like they're in love

and even though I have taken
to fondly calling this My Chubby Summer,
in truth most summers have been this way,
and I'm okay

I'm still okay

so much more
than just okay:

my heart is fat with the ripe fruit of the sun
and its mess in the generous sky.

Serena lies on the bed. She is waiting, again
for me to pay her some attention,
but when I offer my affection, close-up,
purring stops, small paws retreat, head turns away.
She wants me gone. Or is it my fleeting touch she dislikes?
She knows my focus scatters, my busy hands
take flight after a quick fix of warm fur, soft as new buds.
Now, despite my to-do list, I give her
my stilled hand, a quiet beast
to press her cheek against; her breath's
as slow as someone praying – offering
thanks for what's already been accepted.
If I keep my fickle self subdued, she'll offer belly soon,
and I'll be here all blessed afternoon.

INVENTORY

Portage Park, 25 April, 9 a.m.

The geese squabble as they land in the cove
where the last of the winter ducks are fishing
and the mallards and mergansers are paired
and I am the only person on the beach
to witness the sun coming out for the first time in a week.
A heron under the long silver dock
stretches its neck, its beak
catches the light, becomes
a fish. And the young pair of racoons
I startled on the path come crashing through the ivy
like a pair of drunks trying to find a place to piss
along the shore, and from my cold rock perch,
I name these coons Jack and Diane,
just another invasive species
claiming more than is mine, again.
When I head toward home,
I walk under the maples
where this time last year, a pair of young barred owls
told me to get lost, and today the fawn lilies
seem to be averting their eyes, as I do,
from the spray-painted cock and balls on the Douglas Fir.
There are different levels of ownership,
of trying to make one's mark –
just last night I heard the familiar buzz
of the rufous hummingbird, returned to our feeder
after wintering south, and called it mine
even though I know they all sound the same,
and I stared down the doe
eating apple blossoms within reach

of my red tulips that smell like tangerines,
flowers I keep on planting every year
knowing full well the battle I will wage and lose.

EQUANIMITY

November, Sooke River, BC

Salmon fishermen gather at the river's pools,
flick bright lines tipped with flies of neon fuzz and fur

past   seals   eagles   gulls   and snags
to catch the attention of what swims below.

And I am mesmerized by the arcs that mark momentum
from shoulder to wrist – the measured action that makes
    the line fly free.

Then, I let my focus wander, since I'm here
to spend time with my husband, not to snag these dying fish,

and so become fascinated by the rocks beneath me,
heavy and cold, layered and aglitter

and the ancient cedar, top long gone but still growing,
angled toward the river like a tilted head.

The dead chum's silver skin drapes almost elegantly
over stones beside their skeletons, eyes and flesh long gone
    to birds,

the leaves, orange and sepia, are having one last glow
on the ground before becoming the ground,

and the bigleaf maple branches, thickly mossed,
grow ferns like haphazard scales.

Why harass these creatures on their final journey? I don't ask.
I am here to offer company, attention, a gesture of love on
   a sunny morning.

Then, I catch the glint of it, the flash of it,
the thing we're both here to find:

not a fish on a hook but the fishing itself,
moments to act as witness, companion, gatherer,

harvesting the light of a short, clear day
to help us through the coming dark.

A CERTAIN AGE

I, VAJAYJAY: THIRTEEN WAYS

1
In my resting state –
hair in wind,
sunlight on peony.

2
Many words hold power –
I don't need
to labour that point.

3
Taken out of context,
I am   a conch   an orchid   a hole
in the wet earth.

4
Reflected in the fen,
the showy lady's slipper
admires its moody pout.

5
Pussies in poems?
No harm if you titter, no
need to apologize.

6
Triangle, landing strip
or just a little off the top –
vagicians
are standing by.

7
The bed is moving.
The pink canoe
is taking on water.

8
Whisper kitty, kitty.
If you know my secret call,
I will likely come.

9
It's bedtime all day long.
I'm taking song requests
and the beat   just   won't   stop

10
My spam is invitational,
cha-cha and poom-poom
just a click away.

11
Beneath leather, lace, or Lycra,
the portal beacon
still burns bright.

12
Removed
from the poem
I turn inward, dream of tidal pools,
midsummer's kiss.

13
Every Canadian verse
hides the national animal in its mounds:
there's no place like home.

YELLOW BIRCH

I turned seventeen
beneath a canoe
in a thunderstorm, mouth
and hands messing
with love
for a spoiled Italian boy
in silky shorts

Bark Lake Leadership Camp

the same place I wrote
one word
on a giant piece of paper
to describe how I felt
in the forest:
                    small.

This morning, my daughter,
seventeen,
showed up
on my Instagram feed

at a party
                    three thousand miles away.

I am trying to let go.
I should be trying.
I promise to begin;

beneath the birch's
loosened bark

            a second skin.

ZOOM IN

Downtown Vancouver, BC

Look at our solo sunbather
on a cell phone / patio / everyone's Instagram

count the condo towers around her
four mirthless sentries

see her stretch to expose
white inner arms
set herself up with a snack

then gaze at the young trees
little poplars
wearing bright new leaves

watch the cop rerouting traffic
whistle in his mouth

check out the low round building
the centre
of a concrete flower

admire the unfinished high rise
its ombré
of completion levels

the pivoting cranes
with loads a-swinging

78

spy the crow   a flyer
for two-for-one pizza
in its mouth

before you zoom in
on the sunbather
and Snapchat her to your daughter

so she'll make
like the moment
and disappear.

SOIL KING

View Royal, BC

Lightly crying, birthday-style,
as I walk past ripe blackberries
with no container to pick them into,
past   traffic   traffic   traffic
and dying roses
until the Soil King, slinging stones
into a cement trough at the condo build
inspires me to shake off sadness for ten seconds of admiration.

Once there was nothing and then,
a home for twenty families,
and today the twenty men in orange vests
all seem slightly heroic, even if most of them
are standing around at this moment,
watching the dirt make its near-delicate descent.

Earth to earth,
from the Soil King to this building site,
sometimes it's clear that we mostly move matter around,
just kids in a sandbox, delighting
in the simplest elements.

While I clipped the last of the lavender before my walk,
the cat caught a young bird beside me,
but when I yelled, she let it go.
As life faded, the birds' organs blooming
on the sidewalk, I couldn't blame her instinct,
only my lack of awareness at the nature of nature.

And although no one's said a birthday is protected
from such moments, I still expect easy, best-case scenarios,
even if they're the stuff of dreams.
To everyone else at the hip new café I'm writing this in,
it's just another Friday in August, and now that my
iced Earl Grey's long gone, my only companion
is a potted cactus that looks like a rabbit,
its petal ears almost soft enough to touch.

PONDERING DESIRE
IN MIDDLE AGE

Is contentment a choice?
You're already convinced.
My body keeps churning
through any hour or weather.
I may still sink my teeth
into whatever's ripe
but memories of abandon, oblivion,
limbs on limbs in meadows,
are harder to locate.
When I sleep facing in
I put my neck out; I'm afraid
what I offer will wreck my TMJ.
I can't stay focused or stop
yawning; I let the news
shut the whole system down.
Choices seem endless
until I need to make them.
Still, there is only the one ending –
I'll want for nothing
when no longer tangling sheets.
Why can't I hold
both harmony and dreams?
When I ask the hard questions,
the answers are also hard.
I fold myself into child's pose,
joints creaking like old-growth
in yet another storm.

CRADLE THE ROSES

Walking home from the grocery store,
I cradle the roses like they're a newborn –
thorns for rejection, petal mouths for hungry kisses.
I am newlywed / mother / crone,
womb apparently closed like the tightest bud
despite my pleas for flow – in my fiftieth year
on the planet I am no more able to adjust my fate
than when ten or twenty: all prayers fall
like seeds on barren ground.
But are they simply the wrong seeds?
asks my optimistic inner Catholic child.
And isn't a desert alive in its own dusty way?
It is a lot of work, desire. Or do I mean
maintaining the desire of desirability?
When the sweat suit calls out to me, I answer
by climbing right on in. When my lover,
a.k.a. my husband of decades, waits
with my name in his mouth,
I feel my lax belly contract –
so far from foxy and yet
exactly like a fox:
a fox wanting a den, or a hole in the snow
to pounce upon, in search of food.

Five times around the golf course, fresh cedar trail soft as
tears, and the rufous-sided towhees rummaging for leaves
make a sound more mammal than bird. Five times and
then I go deeper into the unmanicured woods, pass a lone
man with a dog, and though I don't know where they
lead, I descend graffitied steps to a narrow creekside trail.
The shush of water washes away the traffic from above
and a whippet appears on the little ivy-skirted path, and
we talk in hushed tones before an older woman follows,
head down. She jumps when she sees me, then smiles
in relief. *You're a black shadow*, she says, and it's true,
I'm decked out in dark shorts and fleece. Every time we
head into the woods we throw dice, hoping we come up
with woman / woman. I'm so tired of this game. The
man I passed had a small poodle – a good sign, I tell
myself. I tell myself lots of things. When my husband
texts me his usual *Good day?* what can I say except
Great? I've gone five times around the golf course, where
a robin quarrelled with a squirrel and people laughed
as they tapped tiny balls into holes in the earth.

My body of work is a body working
the work of a body is to be a body

at work I use my body to work
on other bodies work the body push it   push it good

work out the knots the stress the body gathers
just by being a body at work

the body tightens I work it loose the way
I work with words they grow cell by cell

into a body a whole body of work
animated innervated encapsulated

body blessed or shunned as work
that works on the page in the mouth

by bodies who know words like they're
more than words like the back of their hands

their body the book they know best
love it most when its hairs all stand on end

editor's body says it's still a work in progress
flesh out the ending needs more work.

EASTER SUNDAY SONNET

Hornby Island, BC

We wake to rain and wind and bake-at-home
croissants we brought from Whole Foods, on a whim.
He serves me coffee in a work of art,
the local potter's mug I bought to share.
Outside, small blooms in opera pink bejewel
burnt sienna branches, salmonberry
offering their bling to break the gloom.
What did I bring to hide instead of eggs?
Decades in, there's little I can offer
that he hasn't found or seen already,
and yet, he stays. And yet I stay, each day
another chance to resurrect clichés
of spring love and secret promised candy
to sugar storms both here and still to come.

Become porous
    become the rock at the base of the sacred
    mountain
become, for us
    the wind that ruffles toddler hair
become the pond, the lake, the river
    a body dredged
for us
    become shadow, grey clouds,
puffs of smoke from a doused fire
    for us
become the stream that douses
    our frantic spells and visions
become the speller, the spell keeper, the giver
    for us
become the gift giver, the giver of untaken advice
    – just give 'er,
as in go, fast, get 'er done for us
    become better,
beyond wattles, wobbles, mottled skin
    become memory, perfection
in the past tense, a relic,
    exulted empty space.

Don't we all begin
the day like children,
dishevelled, dream-dipped
and most like ourselves? From
noon to three a.m., a bird
could perch on my daughter's lashes
and she wouldn't bat an eye.
Her curls become sculpture,
public art at the top
of a well-constructed persona
in black and white pants
singing future chart-breakers
to a rapt crowd, but otherwise
she's the same baby
I saw in concert
twenty-three years ago,
weeping in her three-octave range
as I wound up the mechanical swing,
again, me on the floor
as her first audience,
crying too, both of us
unable to fathom
the pain of rupture
as her first tooth
broke through the gum.

THE EMPTY NESTER FINDS PASSION
ON THE PORCH

Wanton now, or completely déshabillé, my florid
faves have lasted a month. Deer knew
of their moment of peak perfection,
leapt my short fence to eat a few
in the front garden, weeks ago, when tender, new.
But these deck-bound, pot-bound crimson tulips
on the back porch have granted me a month
of demure mornings, a month of seductive afternoons.
Their heady fragrance, citrus-vanilla, is long gone now,
but they flash their six-stamened centres, their thickened
pistils, their swollen stigma as if newly born;
how to tell them the party's over? Tonight, despite
every gardener's advice, I'll evict them from these pots,
spent bulbs dangling from still-proud stems.
The bees have turned elsewhere, and so must I.
All eyes are on the hibiscus blooms, sitting among
the fresh leaves like flamenco butterflies,
while the dahlia tubers plead from their paper bag
to be thrust into the newly-vacant, wet, cool dark.

THE EMPTY NESTER,
FIVE YEARS ALONG

This table bears the scars of art,
weeping wax and long division.
And I, the mom, have played my part –
this table bears the scars of art,
paint, packages to send my heart
to my heart, a ceaseless mission.
This table bears the scars of art,
weeping, wax and long division.

First kisses and last hurrahs and honey,
all of them need the tongue.

With a pocket knife and boredom,
a pink pearl eraser begins to resemble art.

Begin to dislocate.
Say it like you mean it.

Show your work.
Does anyone know how?

I bleed scorn when too comfortable.
The past cannot be visited or left.

Despite the weight,
because of the weight

I drag the bag.
Is that normal?

I walk the same path so often
it disappears.

Apropos of everything
I wake,

shuffle forward
into the uncertain, familiar nexts.

Text me when you get there.
Will I ever stop trying to find my way home?

If I squint, if the light is right,
I can see what's here.

DEAR POEM

I am learning to draw the human head. A circle below another circle, rounded or chiselled into a jaw, a chin, then lines to mark the planes of the face and where the sensory organs go. It's just another flower, parts of a botanical specimen pencilled in to honour its existence, and as it is when I examine a blossom up close, I become enraptured by how parts can make a whole. I always draw the eyes too large, the lips too full, the nose too wide, as if I can't believe that all we take in of the world can come through such modest portals. And it's true, the homunculus backs me up: that map of the brain's cortex shows them enlarged to the proportion of what innervation they have. If I learn to draw the rest of the body well, I will need to watch my measurements: you should see the size of its hands.

WITH TREES

After "At Silver Heights,"
Lionel LeMoine Fitzgerald, 1931,
Art Gallery of Ontario

I rarely feel so free in social intercourse with humans
as I always feel with trees.

Lionel LeMoine Fitzgerald,
in a letter to Bertram Brooker, 1937

Everything is impossibly smooth,
as if soaked in hope or prayer –

all the edges gone, even the trees' joints
seem made of young flesh, trunks turning
to torsos, thighs plunged into earth.

The woman in a sunhat is small within
these trunks, secondary but not incidental,
her hand resting tenderly on a slender tree.
Her stance is seductive, comfortable, familiar.

My eye seeks her in the scene
like the breeze does, slides along her arms
to her rounded elbows, shoulders,
her solid, sensual hips, while her gaze
is focused on the soft, small hills
of grass and over the path, to further trees.

I want to know her name – Vally (wife)?
Irene (lover)?
Or, another?

I want to sink deeply
into the natural world, to access,
as Fitzgerald did, whatever unites all beings,
to do as he wanted and make *the painting a living thing*

but mostly I want to be this woman,
hand on sapling, hem pulled by the breeze,
with nothing to do but stand in a summer dress
and interpret a sky of puffy clouds.

LITTLE TRIBUNE BAY

Hornby Island, BC

Likewise is a response I overuse, at the same time, too,
but one hundred per cent, totally, this is what I mean,
all in. I want to jump into a pillowcase and tie it up
from the inside, I want to live between the lines, I want to go
back to the beach and lie half-naked – or is it ninety per cent,
only bottoms un-bared – and let the sun hit me like I'm
charging a weapon, let the salt make patterns on my skin
to tell the sky it matters, and let middle age and pains
and worries over our miraculous machineries shed themselves
like dead scales into the sand when you, my friends
beside me, break from poetry to be the poems and join me
to wade in against the tide, coming in hot.

Save the Cat keeps coming up in conversation,
a book on how to write a novel: fifteen beats
from start to finish and voila – a story that works.
I wonder what might happen if no cats
appeared in the prose, or in the wider world itself?
What if every carnivorous beast ate only flowers
and lolled about in the grass like a pet rabbit? How weak
would the plot become without teeth or chase or death?
In my own work-in-progress I have saved no one,
but six years after the discovery of a one-centimetre dragon,
slayed before it devoured the breast in which it hid,
no fire or scales have been detected.
Just this week, a single red and frilly bloom
on the hibiscus plant I was given
as solace that day the beast was first discovered
appeared like a self-aggrandizing metaphor
on the very morning of the all-clear scan.
And just to round out the story with some further
    pathetic fallacy,
my tabby cat adores this plant, even though – or because –
it contains a mild toxin that may cause hallucinations.
Once a blossom falls, she carries it around the house
like a dead bird, pleased as any predator.
I know, I know, I should keep this plant far from my feline,
but how can I take this small, rare pleasure from her
    wild-free life?
Wait. I hear a thunk, just now: the bloom has fallen.
It's a race to grab it before she does, but I make it,
I beat her to it, and take a moment to appreciate
the symbolism of its still-strong pistil, raised like a
    middle finger,
before I compost the flower and save the cat, again.

THE BLOCKED WRITER LOOKS
TO THE GARDEN

The mock orange announces itself
like a debutante on the staircase
and all faces turn toward its light.

And still, it's not enough.

Even though in this moment
summer has arrived, the season
I proclaim, over and over, to be *my* season,
even though, in this moment, I feel happy,
I am still left wanting.

Do I think writing will make me happy?
What if that isn't the goal?
What if it's honesty? Am I winning?
If so, is it a contest?

I chase the deer from the garden;
I string nets over the tender shoots and buds;
I keep planting what they love.

If there's a metaphor here, I'm ignoring it.
If this is wasting my life –

The mock orange doesn't mean to mock me,
though I feel the sting of its thousand blooms.

And what of it? All perfume, no fruit,
and I love it anyway.

When will I turn that grace upon myself?

Was it you who woke me at five a.m.?
Or was it my husband's blood sugar alarm
my Mafioso dreams
my overproofing sourdough
my fear of deer eating the tulip buds
my unfiled taxes
my mother's health
my aching neck
my anxiety hangover
my jaw trying to grind it all away?
Or was it this sunrise
caught in the birdbath,
the Japanese apricot tree in blossom,
the new leaves on the climbing rose?
Was it another funny animal video
sent by my daughter, a hedgehog
taking a bath, a fox, laughing?
Was it the birdsong, April-strong,
or the strawberries to slice for breakfast
into a chartreuse pottery bowl,
their cold sweetness what I'll remember,
not the seeds in my teeth?
Was it, dear poem, all of this
and more? Tell me, again,
is there enough room
in this spacious moment
and fleeting life
to hold it all?

THIS IS THE DOOR
YOU'VE BEEN LOOKING FOR

Portage Park, View Royal, BC

If this small suburban park
hides a door into another world

just behind the nettles
gathering light and rain to fuel their sting

under the green bench
spattered with petals

then the trees hide a door
leading to another door

opening onto a room made of wood
and dogtooth violets

where a woman feels the breeze
injecting spring straight into her blood.

This last hidden door
is as small as a silver raindrop

reflecting a cloud
as big as a whole new planet

and it opens
like a flower does for a bee

and she
if the woman is me

wears it 'round her neck
for safekeeping

and safe travels
through whatever's yet to come.

The section "Birding at Night" is in memory of my paternal grandmother, Dorothy Marguerite Paul (1926–2018).

"The Day before the Wake" received an honourable mention for *Arc Magazine*'s Award of Awesomeness, May 2023.

The first line of "Before the Divorce" is from Elizabeth Bishop's poem "Arrival at Santos," in *Poems* (New York: Farrar, Straus and Giroux, 2011).

"Montreal, You Eat Our Young" was drafted at John Barton's sonnet workshop at the GVPL.

The epigraph in "Cridgeon" comes from Elizabeth Bishop's poem "Paris, 7 a.m.," in *Poems* (New York: Farrar, Straus and Giroux, 2011).

The epigraph for "Endemic" comes from Charles Darwin, *The Voyage of the Beagle* (London, New York, Dutton: Dent, 1959).

"Autophagy": autophagy is "the action of feeding upon oneself; *spec.* metabolic consumption of the body's own tissue, as in starvation or certain diseases" (https://www. oed.com/dictionary/autophagy_n).

The first line of "Household Haunting" is from Elizabeth's Bishop's poem "House Guest," in *Poems* (New York: Farrar, Straus and Giroux, 2011).

"AWP 2020 Event T 150: The Pocket Epic: Poets Writing at Length" is dedicated to Yvonne Blomer and Christine Walde, who were there, and to the poets who presented their work at the event: Sumita Chakraborty, Melissa Crow, Meg Day, and Paisley Rekdal.

A version of "What Humans Do" originally appeared in the *Poems from Planet Earth* anthology, edited by Yvonne Blomer and Cynthia Woodman Kerkham (Vancouver Island: Leaf Press, 2013).

The poem "Greener Grass Mash-up" was inspired by e.e. cummings, William Blake, T.S. Eliot, Langston Hughes, E.M. Forster, Theodore Roethke, William Shakespeare, Walt Whitman, Carolyn Forche, Lou Reed, Gil Scott-Heron, ABBA, and Avery Jane, as well as *Three Billy Goats Gruff*, *Little Red Riding Hood*, and the folk song *My Bonnie*.

A version of "Maybe it was the Grass-Fed Butter" was published in *Vallum* 20, no. 1.

"Spring Sonnet for Tabby Cat" was published in *Gyroscope Review* (Spring 2023).

"I, Vajayjay, Thirteen Ways" first appeared in *Grain Magazine* 46, no. 2.

"Dice" appeared in *Quartet Journal* 3, no. 2.

"Work Body Work" owes its existence to my decades-long career as a registered massage therapist. Still going strong!

"With Trees" is an ekphrastic poem based on one of my favourite works of art: *At Silver Heights*, by Lionel LeMoine Fitzgerald. I first saw this painting at the AGO as a teenager and have held onto a postcard of it ever since, which lives on my office wall. The epigraph is from Michael Parke-Taylor, *Lionel LeMoine Fitzgerald: Life & Work* (Toronto: The Canadian Art Library and Art Canada Institute, 2019).

"Little Tribune Bay" is dedicated to Andrea S., Catherine S., and Carmen M.

"The Blocked Writer Looks to the Garden" is after James Wright's "Lying in a Hammock at William Duffy's Farm in Pine Island, Minnesota," in *The Branch Will Not Break* (Middletown, CT: Wesleyan University Press, 1963).

ACKNOWLEDGMENTS

I am grateful to have had the privilege of creating these poems on Vancouver Island, the traditional and unceded territory of the ləkʷəŋən-speaking peoples, today known as the Esquimalt and Songhees Nations; Tiohtià:ke (Montreal), the unceded Indigenous lands of the Kanien'kehá:ka/Mohawk Nation; and the unceded traditional Omàmìwininì (Algonquin) territory in Lanark County, Ontario.

Thank you to everyone at McGill-Queen's University Press, for bringing this collection to life, with extra thanks to Carolyn Smart for her encouraging, insightful editing.

A number of these poems began in Yvonne Blomer's fantastic online Monday evening poetry classes over the pandemic years. I have so much gratitude for the supportive community she's created, and for her keen and thoughtful edits. Thanks to my poetic comrades in the Electronic Garret, and the women in my writing groups, the Fiction Bitches and the WWC, all of whom have played a part in bringing some of these poems to their final form. Special appreciation for writers and friends Traci Skuce, Jenny Vester, Karen Chester, Danielle Janess, Christine Walde, Andrea Scott, and Yvonne Blomer, for their generative and regenerative support. And a big group hug to my Pussy Posse, a group of strong, vibrant women who have been supporting each other through thick and thin for over twenty years.

My family, as always, has provided a creative, supportive base from which to write, and for this I am eternally thankful. Ryan, your unfailing belief in me is a treasure beyond measure. Avery Jane, thank you for living by example as you follow your passion and share your music with the world, and for sharing your Montreal home with me for creative getaways and fun visits. To my parents, siblings, and extended family, I offer my deep appreciation for your support and generosity; having a writer in the family isn't for the faint of heart.

Over the years both the BC Arts Council and the Canada Council for the Arts have offered funding for my writing projects, and I am grateful for these programs that help to support artists in Canada.